SHORTCUTS
To GOD

CONTENTS

ACKNOWLEDGMENTS

I wish to share my deep and loving appreciation to my wife, Diane Cirincione, and to my dear friend, Hal Zina Bennett, for all of their loving encouragement and editorial assistance with this book. I wish to thank Gloria and Ken Wapnick, of the Foundation for A Course in Miracles for their permission to quote from the Course. There are times when I have paraphrased the Course according to my understanding. I have indicated any direct quotes from the Course with endnotes.

We experience God
when we see only the light
in everyone we meet.

DEDICATION

I dedicate this book, with boundless love
and gratefulness, to God, my grand-
children—Jacquelyn, Grant, Jalena,
and Lexie—to all the children who have
come to the CENTERS FOR ATTITUDINAL
HEALING, and to the children of the world
who teach us all what unconditional love,
light, and innocence, are all about.
They give life to the statement,
"And a little child shall lead them."

CELESTIAL ARTS
P.O. Box 7123
Berkeley, California 94707

Celestial Arts titles are distributed in Canada by Ten Speed Canada, in
the United Kingdom and Europe by Airlift Books, in South Africa by
Real Books, in Australia by Simon & Schuster Australia, in New
Zealand by Southern Publishers Group, and in Southeast Asia by
Berkeley Books.

Portions from *A Course in Miracles*® Copyright 1975, 1992, 1999,
reprinted by permission of THE FOUNDATION FOR A COURSE IN MIRACLES,
1275 Tennanah Lake Road, Roscoe, NY 12776-5905
The ideas represented herein are the personal interpretation
and understanding of the author and are not necessarily endorsed
by the copyright holder of *A Course in Miracles*®

Cover and text design by Leslie Cabarga

Library of Congress Cataloging-in-Publication Data
Jampolsky, Gerald G., 1925-
    Shortcuts to GOD : finding peace quickly through
practical spirituality / Gerald G. Jampolsky ;
foreword by Hugh Prather ; illustrated by Leslie Cabarga.
       p. cm.
Sequel to: Love is letting go of fear.
Includes bibliographical references.
ISBN 0-89087-953-2 (pbk.)
1. Spiritual life. 2. Mental healing. 1. Title.
BL624 .J436 2000
291.4'4--dc21   00-024124

First printing, 2000
Printed in Canada

1 2 3 4 5 6 7 8 — 05 04 03 02 01 00

SHORTCUTS To GOD

GERALD G. JAMPOLSKY, M.D.

Foreword by
Hugh Prather

Illustrated by
Leslie Cabarga

CELESTIAL ARTS
Berkeley, California

PART IV

Epilogue

AUTHOR'S NOTE

Most of my life, in spite of efforts to the contrary, I took the wrong roads and the long cuts through life, never the short cuts. Being dyslexic I confused right and left. If I tried to follow someone's directions, I invariably ended up going in the wrong direction, adding hours to my journey. I was a master at doing things the hard way.

In my younger days my friends called me "Wrong Way Jampolsky," a nickname borrowed from "Wrong Way Corrigan," a man who flew across the Atlantic, telling authorities that the reason he did it was that he got lost.

Feeling lost has been an unpleasant theme during a great deal of my life. It's been easy to blame getting lost on my dyslexia. But I now think it had more to do with my stubborn ego's fight with God. Now, having gained some expertise about taking long cuts, I feel I have gained some insights about short cuts as well.

During so much of my past I have been like a rudderless boat going around in circles. At long last I feel that I have a rudder and know where I want to go—and that is the direction of going home to God. Most of my life this was certainly not my goal! As a child I was confused about God, partly because I frequently read the word God backwards, so it came out as "dog."

Most of my early adult life I was a militant atheist, running away from God, denying God's existence, fighting with God, and blaming God for the many awful things that happened to me. If God came up in a conversation at a party, I left that conversation and fled as far to the opposite side of the room as I could.

In spite of many achievements in my life, I still felt empty inside. My success with outer goals did not bring me the happiness and peace I was seeking. It never occurred to me that what I was looking for was the God-Self that was inside me and that I had never really been separate from God.

In 1975, following a painful divorce that ended my twenty-year marriage, and ending a long period of alcoholism, I consciously chose a spiritual path and started healing my relationship with God. That same year I helped to found the CENTER FOR ATTITUDINAL HEALING, now located in Sausalito, California, which in turn helped to inspire the growth of over 150 Centers or groups around the world, all of which offer free services to people who are faced with catastrophic illness and their family members. Additionally, these Centers offer free support to people in all walks of life interested in using Attitudinal Healing to deal with personal, as well as professional challenges.

That same year, I was also introduced to *A Course in Miracles*, which radically changed my life, helping me listen to the voice of Love rather than the voice of fear.

All the books I have written were inspired by my heart's resonating with the heartbeat of God which I found in *A Course in Miracles*. In 1979, I wrote my first book, *Love is Letting Go of Fear*. I only used the word

"God" once in that book. Though that book was about spiritual transformation, I avoided the word God because I still didn't feel comfortable with it in my vocabulary. Any time I used it, it seemed to stick in my throat.

Today I look at things differently. In writing this book—a sequel to *Love is Letting Go of Fear*, some twenty-plus years later—it is as if I have been guided to write a book about remembering God.

This book is about finding the shortcuts that will lead us to God regardless of the theological or philosophical paths we use to get there. It is about removing the obstacles we have placed in our own paths. It is about knowing and experiencing God.

—*January 2000, Kailua, Hawaii*

FOREWORD

By Hugh Prather

To some readers, *Shortcuts to God* might smack of the quick fix, or an oversimplification, such as we find in all too many self-help books. However, suggesting that there are shortcuts to God is actually an understatement. God is total simplicity. God is One. God is without time, change or uncertainty. And although God's unity and oneness is pure Love, the ego (or small mind) looks at God anxiously, seeing simplicity as the end of all it wants us to think.

Having known Jerry for over twenty years, and having observed him working with countless people in extreme distress, I know his deep inner simplicity is the real thing. You will feel its source as you read this book. In almost every line is the resonance of a united soul and of sincere words honestly lived. It's a book that flows from pure intent, expressed daily in a thousand small ways. Just as I did, you will probably feel, "Here is a place where God is known. Here are beliefs that come from the heart."

Jerry's book *Love Is Letting Go of Fear* took us to the gate; *Shortcuts to God* takes us over the threshold. It states bluntly what a young psychiatrist, even then a world-renown lecturer and noted author of professional journal articles, was understandably hesitant to put into print in the late 1970s. I remember Jerry's eleventh hour decision to substitute the word Love for the word God in his manuscript, a compassionate change for readers of that day.

You'll note in this book that Jerry uses the word God freely throughout, but it is in a way that is welcoming, not discriminating, inclusive, not polarizing. God is revealed as a gentle, all-encompassing Love, embracing you and me and every living being, leaving no one out of the loop. The God that Jerry describes is not only within the heart of each of us but is the heart of each of us. God is the higher power, the inner power, the only power.

Immersed in God, Jerry stains everyone he meets with large spots of light and smudges of warmth. Children crawl up on his lap and at night cats sleep on his chest. He is not flawless—none of us are—but certainly he is a window through which God's light shines easily. In this book he explains how everyone can wipe the pane clean.

Jerry originated Attitudinal Healing, and free Attitudinal Healing Centers, for children and adults with catastrophic conditions, as well as many other life challenges. Independent Centers now exist throughout the world. Although tied to no religious doctrine, Attitudinal Healing is a spiritual approach. Jerry's training, however, was in Freudian-based child psychiatry. Someone who can make the transition from board diplomat in psychiatry with a medical degree from Stanford, to helping children through turning to Love—and not even charging for it—either is insane or should be a candidate for the Nobel Peace Prize. Yet, Jerry is one of the sanest voices on the planet.

The professional risks of making the switch from Freud to God should be obvious, yet today, Jerry and his wife Diane Cirincione, a Ph.D. in clinical psychology, are sought world-wide by traditional hospital and medical centers as trainers and teachers of the Attitudinal Healing approach. They have worked together in over fifty countries. I emphasize this in case there is any doubt that a God-centered teaching in a medical center can be practical.

I remember well the first startling example I saw of just how practical and effective Jerry's approach is. My wife Gayle and I met Jerry in 1978, soon after he started the first Center for Attitudinal Healing in Tiburon, California. Later that year I attended the Center's first Christmas party. Jerry picked me up at the airport and took me to the building where it was being held. As I went through the door I was unprepared for what I saw. It was as if I had walked into a war zone hospital.

Filling the room were kids on crutches, with amputated limbs, kids in wheelchairs too crippled by disease to stand, blind or partially paralyzed kids from brain injuries, and bald kids drained of color from chemotherapy. But I immediately sensed that there was something out of place in the room. It took me several seconds to absorb the fact that almost all of these children were very happy, that they were talking animatedly, and—above all—they were laughing!

Jerry asked me to come with him to meet a teenage girl who was conversing with two adults. As we walked toward her, he told me that until recently she had been a fashion model who was thought to have great promise. Then a car crash paralyzed the left side of her body. She was standing up with the help of crutches that clasped her arms above and below her elbows, and I noticed that she couldn't let go of them to shake hands or hold a drink. Although her speech was slurred, she could make herself understood fairly well. But as the four of us were chatting she suddenly lost her balance and fell straight backwards. She hit the wooden floor so hard that several people ran over to help her. Once we had her back on her feet, this former model smiled, her eyes moist with pain, and she said, "Well, at least I'm finally getting a hard butt!"

Over the months to come, Gayle and I had the opportunity to get to know a number of the children and their parents. Later, Jerry and I traveled with some of them on a lecture tour. For the next three years, Jerry and I visited children's hospitals in various parts of the country, teaching kids mental imagery exercises to lessen their pain and promote healing.

I have seen first hand the effects of Jerry's approach so many times and under so many different conditions that I can assure you that the words in this book are indeed "shortcuts to God." Of course, that also means shortcuts to happiness, purposefulness, and deeply felt peace. If even very young and very sick children can grasp and lean on these concepts, anyone can. This is not just another feel-good book about love and forgiveness. It is a deeply practical book, born in the fire of tragedy. It can guide you to connect to your spiritual Source, heal your relationships, cultivate your compassion, open your heart to love, hear your own guidance, and live a richer, happier, and above all simpler life.

INTRODUCTION

Several years ago my wife Diane Cirincione and I were in New Jersey lecturing. Afterwards, we were having dinner with friends, who shared the following story with us:

A friend of our friend had recently brought home their new baby, their second child. One evening their three year old daughter said she wanted to go into the baby's room alone.

At first reluctant because they feared there might be some sibling rivalry, the parents finally granted their daughter her wish. Besides with the intercom they had in the baby's room they could listen in on and make sure everything was okay.

As their daughter tiptoed up to the baby's crib, they heard their her softly say: "Baby, remind me what God is like. I am beginning to forget."

What was true for that child is true for so many of us adults. Our memory of God has dimmed. We live in a world that has become fearful of God, fearful of love, fearful of trusting a Higher Power, and fearful of trusting ourselves or each other. Perhaps not remembering God is our primary problem in life.

*"Baby, remind me what God is like.
I am beginning to forget."*

This book is about lifting the fog of amnesia that cloud ancient memories of our Higher Power. Though we may have temporarily lost our faith and trust in our Source, it abides deep within our hearts, waiting for us to remember.

This book is about remembering. It is about choosing to forget our hurts and pains and everything else that may have blocked God's Love, which surrounds us at all times.

Though I talk about God in these pages it is not about theology or religion. Rather, it is about what I

"I AM the Rainbow!"

call practical spirituality. My hope is that what I've written here will point the way for using spiritual principles in every area of our lives.

Twenty-five years ago I never would have believed anyone who told me I would one day be on a spiritual path, much less write a book about God. And I am sure there are readers who will think it is strange for a man who was an atheist most of his life to be writing about shortcuts to God.

I find that I am not alone in having spent much of my adult life either angry at God or believing that God did not exist. To me the world seemed chaotic and unfair, always out of control. It was clear I could not control what happens in the world, and I believed that God couldn't either.

My beliefs about God vacillated constantly. At times I felt like God was completely arbitrary but arbitrary or not, God had surely abandoned me. I believed that if I wanted to get anything from life it was all up to me. Nobody was there to help me.

Like so many others, I spent my time trying to find the pot of gold and goodies at the end of the rainbow. Today I no longer look for the pot of gold because I recognize that the rainbow IS the pot of gold—and you and I are the rainbow.

Looking back on my first 50 years of life, it seems I had a very demanding ego, fixated on trying to control others. The last thing I was interested in was letting go of my control issues and letting a God that I did not trust be in charge!

My fear of God started at an early age. When I was

eight years old my parents told me that God would strike me dead if I ever ate bacon. At a Cub Scout meeting I ate bacon for the first time, and immediately started looking around to see if God was really going to strike me dead. The fact that I wasn't dead proved to me that there was no God.

I began to believe that people who believed in God were fearful and were not using their intellects. I had not the slightest clue that I was the fearful one.

It was not until I was around 50 that I began to realize that my emptiness, depression, agitation and unhappiness were all due to a hunger in my soul, a longing to be fulfilled and connected with my Source.

Many of us who have been disappointed by some of the things we have been told in our religious training. Or we have felt disillusioned or even betrayed because people who taught us about religion did not seem to walk their talk. The result was that we got hurt and lost our trust and faith. These feelings tended to cause a separation between ourselves and God.

Perhaps the first shortcut to take is having a willingness to go beyond the word God. Maybe we can't define God but we can certainly experience God. To allow such an experience we need to let go of any past perceptions.

I am convinced that the length of the journey, whether long or short, depends on our belief system. Because of my split-mind there have been many times that I listened to the voice of my ego and chose conflict rather than peace. I didn't realize that my personality self, my ego, perceived God and peace of mind as enemies.

*"When you are ambivalent it is difficult
to experience the peace of God."*

There have been many times when I thought I was trying to open the door to God but realized later that my own foot was holding that door closed. It is my impression that many people suffer from this same error, one that comes from our self-attacking ambivalence in our relationship with God.

We can choose to move our feet away from that door, allowing ourselves to experience the Presence of an unconditionally loving God and feel a sense of oneness with God and all others.

The insights and lessons in these pages are much more about unlearning than they are about learning. They are about letting go of being in a hurry, of making our intellects our gods, and being self-absorbed in the past and future, where God is never found. It is about letting go of the daily things that keep us separate from God, such as our obsessions to control and change other people, to blame others and condemn ourselves.

Above all it is about getting out of the way so that we can surrender to Love.

I believe that somewhere deep inside all of us, whether we are conscious of it or not, is a longing to experience a joining and an enduring peace with each other and with that Peaceful Presence that created us. Sooner or later we will all come to experience that Presence ...and we can all choose to make it sooner rather than later.

Instinctively we all know that the shortest shortcut to God is to recognize that we are already home in the Heart of God. So there is no need for either shortcuts

*"When we choose to see the light in others
we then experience it in ourselves."*

or longcuts because in reality there is no journey to take at all!

Keep the door open to God and you will experience the natural state of our hearts where a bright Light from the flame of love never goes out, where there is passion to be fully alive and compassion for all that lives. When we choose to take shortcuts to

God we free ourselves to remember that we are the Light of the World. With that vision each of us can find the Light of God in everything around us.

In contrast to when I wrote *Love is Letting Go of Fear*, I can now identify with Carl Jung who, when asked if he believed in God, confidently replied: "No, my relationship is beyond belief. I now have come to know God."

I now listen and talk with God all day long. Each day is filled with God Talk. I do my best, though not always successfully, to make all my choices based on listening to the Inner Voice of God. It is my goal that my will and God's would be one and the same.

I still need all the help I can get. For example the screen saver on my computer has one of my favorite quotes:

"The Peace of God is shining in me now."[6]

This book is for people like me who still find themselves struggling in life, who know in their hearts that there must be a better way, and who are willing to seek that better way by learning to step aside and let God lead the way.

PART I

The PURPOSE of LIFE

When we choose to believe that our purpose is to love and forgive, we begin to experience life's deeper meaning. Giving and receiving become one. The act of giving, choosing to be helpful to others without expecting anything in return, allows us to experience the Presence of God and to know that we are extensions of God's Love. The more that we choose to live in the present, the more we experience God.

We can choose to see our purpose in life as messengers of love, messengers of God. And if we want

"If you want to call God, it makes no difference which telephone booth you use."

to make a call to God, it really doesn't matter which telephone booth we use.

Our egos are convinced that their purpose in life is to make judgments, to attack, to create conflict, to be unforgiving, to see chaos and scarcity instead of inner peace and abundance. When we act from our egos, our actions are based on fear of love and fear of God, and we become messengers of judgment, anger, hate, and destruction.

This is because the purpose of the ego is get rather

than give. Its appetite is unending. No matter how much we acquire or hold on to, it is never enough.

We lose all memory of God when we listen to the voice of ego, the voice of fear. Because our egos see God and peace as enemies, they will do what they can to delude us into thinking there is no God. They would then have us make material possessions, financial security, and money our gods.

TAKING A NEW LOOK AT OUR PERCEPTIONS OF GOD

Childhood Images of God

What we think God is or isn't, how we attempt to define God, and how we experience God, will be very different for each person. Sometimes, our picture of God is a kind of projection of

our physical self and the physical world we live in.

The image of God I had as a child was that of a giant with a long white robe, white hair and a long, flowing, white beard. He was wise and all knowing, looking down at me from the sky. He was always frowning, judging and, according to my parents, ready to punish me if I did anything wrong.

Since I did not see myself doing much of anything that God would consider good, I always felt that punishment must be just around the corner for me. I lived in an almost constant state of fear, wondering what awful things God had in store for me. I was sure God would punish me for being the kind of child that could do nothing right. Whenever I brought home a poor report card I was sure God was going to drop a brick right on my head.

Though hidden from my awareness, I believe I carried these same childhood fears of being judged, attacked, and abandoned by God into my adulthood.

I had such strong judgments against God that I decided that anyone who believed in God must be full of fear. If they used their intellect, they too would do the only sensible thing there was to do—which was to discard their belief in God.

WHO ABANDONED WHOM?

It was not until many years later that I discovered that I was the fearful one. I had things backwards. It was not that God had abandoned me but that I had abandoned God!

If we find that we are still carrying around with us a childhood image of God that does not bring us peace, this may be an opportune time to heal that mistaken perception.

FACE OF GOD TODAY

Today, I no longer have a negative reaction to the word God. But I do find the word itself limiting because my experience of the Presence of God is beyond what any words could possibly explain. The closest word I can think of is "awe."

The mystery of God remains beyond the comprehension of my intellect and imagination. And since God is not linear, neither is my experience of this loving Source in any way analytical.

No matter what words we might use to describe that which created us, more and more of us are changing our perceptions about God. Many believe that there is an unconditionally loving Source that connects us all as one and which is beyond time, space, and the perceptions of our physical senses.

For me the experience of Love and Joy is beyond time and space and is outside anything that has to do with the physical senses. It is where nothing exists but never-ending Love, a reality where Love is all there is and everything that there is.

When I am able to experience my oneness with God, it is as if my soul is resonating with all the love in the universe, where everything is joined and there is no separation. This experience continues to be beyond my imagination or intellectual comprehension.

For me remembering and experiencing the Presence of God comes from trusting and having faith in a Loving, Creative Source that has infinite intelligence and wisdom. It is a Source without gender and without form. It is a force of compassionate and unconditional Love and Light that continues to love us and comfort us and be ever present.

TO BE PEACEFUL YOU DO NOT HAVE TO BELIEVE IN GOD

It is important to recognize that one does not have to believe in God or use the word "God" to experience Oneness. The moment our egos or intellects come into play, and we attempt to put words around our concepts of God, a feeling of separation from one another and from God can begin to take place.

I have found that many people profess that they do not believe in God. Yet, after spending time with them I frequently discover that, while they do not believe in the God they were told about in their childhoods, they do believe there is something greater than themselves, some undefinable force that created them. They live their lives with kindness, gentleness, tenderness, compassion, and caring, free of any need to judge others. To me their lives are "Godly," though they will deny any belief in God and certainly would not use these words to describe themselves.

What is important is not the words we use to describe God but rather our thoughts and actions, that is, how we live and experience our lives. When we believe that the essence of our being is Love, and that our true identity is spiritual, we start to understand why all of our relationships are opportunities to see the Light of Love in one another and to know that what we see is a reflection of who we are. It is then that we begin to notice our experience of God being manifest in all our relationships. And it is also then that each of us may realize that we are the light that shines the darkness away.

Who Am I?

As long as we think that who we are is limited to our body, we are taking the long road home to God. If we think that who we are is limited to our personality self, or ego, or to the role we play in our family, at work or in society, we will remain spiritually empty.

*"I Am the Light That
Shines Away the Darkness."*

The first principle of Attitudinal Healing is that
the essence of our being is love. When we are willing
to shift our perception, to believe that our true self
is a spiritual being temporarily inhabiting a body,
we begin to recognize and experience our oneness
with God.

"Love is all there is
and everything there is."

We begin to recognize that as spiritual, non-physical beings we are eternal. Who and what we are is love, a love that never dies, and a love whose light can never be extinguished. It's a reality where love is everything there is and the only thing there is.

As we remind ourselves of our purpose, of who and what we really are as spiritual beings, we feel more in harmony with the universe, extending unconditional love and forgiveness to all of those around us. Our awareness of our Oneness becomes increasingly apparent and our illusions of separation begin to disappear. It is then that we begin to notice our experience of God manifesting in all our relationships.

We can change our belief system and heal any misperceptions we might have. In preparing ourselves to take a shortcut to God, we need to have a willingness to change our belief system and look at the possibility of our changing the misperceptions of God that we may be holding on to.

Forgetting and Remembering

Has it ever occurred to you that going through life we have possibly focused on the wrong things to remember and have forgotten what is most important?

Many of us go through life with a long laundry list of the hurts, traumas and injustices we have suffered in life. If we hold onto this list it will only remind us to scratch the old wounds and keep them bleeding.

By practicing what is called "celestial amnesia," it is possible to forget the old pain and even wipe away the scars. Celestial amnesia is the practice of remembering only the Love that God continues to give to us and the love that we extend to others. It is a shortcut to God and to a way of remembering the presence of God's Love.

We might do this by imagining that someone gives us a special medicinal tea to drink that causes us to forget all the past hurts in our lives. As soon as you drink it, all your memories of a painful past vanish. In their place you only remember the love you have given and received. For a moment, just imagine how that would be. Imagine yourself drinking this special tea and experiencing its benefits, knowing you can do this in your mind any time you wish to release yourself from the past.

IT'S TIME TO STOP BLAMING GOD

If something goes wrong in our life, even if we do not believe in God, there is a great temptation to blame somebody—and God is frequently the one we blame most.

If a child we know becomes seriously ill or is killed in an accident, if we or a loved one develops cancer, or if we are witness to terrible tragedies that nobody can explain, we frequently make God the fall guy.

Insurance companies play a part in this belief system by writing into their policies that they will not pay for certain losses, such as a house being destroyed in a flood, because it is what they call an "Act of God."

Isn't it high time that we stopped giving God a bad rap and begin to recognize that God does not cause bad things to happen to us, although it is certainly true that in the insane world we live in many things do happen that defy our understanding.

OUR UNFORGIVING THOUGHTS ABOUT GOD AND OUR RELIGIOUS TRAINING

I am convinced that one of the things that kept me separate from God was my unforgiving thoughts about my religious training and the religious teachers that I had who did not walk their talk. I also had unforgiving thoughts about a God who I believed did terrible things.

For many years there was a place inside me that was fearful of being attacked by a judgmental God, who was the only God I knew. I felt guilty about countless things, but buried in my unconscious were guilty feelings about my separating myself from God. The result was that I ran away from God and from religion.

There are countless men and women who continue to find solace in their different places of worship. Yet, millions of others leave their churches, synagogues, mosques, or other places of worship, because they do not find spirituality in these places. Many become disillusioned because they do not believe in the judgmental or punishing image of God they were taught as children.

Others lose faith when they discover that their religious teachers do not walk their talk but instead are involved in sexual, physical, and psychological abuse. This has resulted in large numbers of people abandoning their religious institutions and not just walking but sometimes even running away from God.

Some of these people have felt like lost souls who were wandering through life with a sense of spiritual emptiness.

There are still others who have chosen to embark upon a spiritual journey. Many such seekers do not want to be categorized in any way. They say, "I am going home to God in my own way and do not need the dogma of any religious organization to tell me how to do it." They want to be free souls, and their numbers are increasing even as the memberships of many religious institutions are decreasing.

FORGIVING GOD AND OUR RELIGIOUS TRAINING

At our Center for Attitudinal Healing we have observed that many people choose to let go of their old concepts of God and heal their relationships with their previous places of worship. They have returned to their churches, mosques, or synagogues. For some this requires that they let go of their perceptions about their religious training and the persons they felt had hurt them.

Speaking for myself, forgiving my misperceptions about God, my religious training, and some of my teachers as well, has thrown the door wide open for me to begin experiencing a loving God.

*When we are depressed,
somewhere deep inside,
we are denying
the Presence of God.*

PART II

A MAP of

GOD ♡ EXPRESS

SHORTCUTS to GOD

Most of us have had the experience of being on a journey and stopping to ask for directions. Sometimes there is a person who will show us our location on a map, then describe certain landmarks we'll see as we travel toward our destination. These landmarks will assure us that we are going in the right direction. They are truly comforting when we are heading into territories that are foreign to us.

The purpose of Part Two is to provide this kind of assistance on your journey, to describe certain landmarks that can help you stay on the pathway and reassure you that you are moving steadily toward your destination.

The following writings are landmarks. If you are watching for them along the way, you can be assured that you are on a shortcut to God.

Counting Our Blessings

When we are aware of counting our blessings every moment of the day we can be assured that we are on the right road. Counting your blessings means refusing to see anything that might be happening to you as a punishment.

Every experience in our lives can be looked upon as bringing us closer to love and closer to God. It is pos-

*"Counting your blessings
instead of your hurts."*

sible to see all of life's experiences as positive lessons that God would have us learn. We may not be able to see what those lessons are right away but by simply holding this belief in our minds they are often revealed. We can choose to count only our blessings and not our hurts.

A shortcut to remembering God is to make two simple words our mantra for life: *Thank you!*

*"Let me see the value
in quieting my mind."*

In the world of the ego, we are taught to believe that we must count every hurt and always be preoccupied with them. Our egos seem to have an irresistible urge to scratch the scars of these old wounds and keep them bleeding so that we will never forget. Because, once again, the goal of the ego is suffering, not joy, and conflict rather than peace.

Every moment of our lives we have a choice: We can count our blessings or count our hurts. Which would you choose? One is a landmark that tells that you are on a direct road, a shortcut to God. The other is a landmark telling you that you are on the long, complicated journey of the ego, with pain, suffering, and conflict.

GRATTITUDE

When we are on the road of love and forgiveness, gratitude becomes a way of life. To feel gratitude in each moment is a sure sign that we have not only found a shortcut to God, but that boundless Love is with us and within us at all times. When we heal our perceptions of anger, suffering and grievance, we can be thankful, assured that everything which happens to us can bring us closer to that which created us.

STILLING OUR MINDS

Stillness of the mind helps keep us on the shortcut to God. Some people find this stillness through meditating or in moments of prayer. It is through these that they find a connection with God.

I like repeating the Native American saying:

A busy mind is a sick mind.

A slow mind is a healthy mind.

A still mind is a divine mind.

The chatter of our minds can drown out our memory of God. Often that chatter consists of conflicting goals, where one part of our mind is fighting with another part.

When we get caught between our own mind chatter and the often conflicting messages of the busyness of everyday life, it can seem almost impossible to experience peace. It is then that we begin to lose sight of our path.

When our mind is still, like a calm, quiet mountain lake, we can see everything with perfect clarity and with no obstacles. When our mind loses its stillness and gets lost in its own chatter, the still lake becomes muddy and our vision becomes clouded. It is then that we tend to lose our connection with our Higher Power.

The quiet voice of God is best heard when our minds are as still as a clear mountain lake.

When you at last see the value of stilling your mind and no longer being obsessively busy, you can be assured that you have passed a landmark telling you that you are on a shortcut to God.

FOLLOWING YOUR HEART

Following our heart shortens the way home, to the home that we never really left.

Our ego would like us to make our intellect our god, because the ego knows that the intellect is not capable of experiencing Love or God.

Experiencing God is not an intellectual process. When we make our brain and our intellect our gods, we no longer remember God. We become glued to what our intellect and our physical senses tell us is real.

Our ego deceives us into believing that if something cannot be measured and replicated then it is not scientifically sound and therefore not worthy of being accepted. Moreover, it would have us believe that only that which has a physical form is real.

One often hears the statement, "If I can not see God with my own eyes, then God must not exist, is not real, and is only an illusion."

The last thing our egos would want us to believe

"Right from the start, follow your heart."

or have faith in would be something that we cannot touch with our hands or see with our eyes.

Unfortunately God flunks the test when it comes to these criteria.

Our egos would have us forget that God is an experience of the heart and soul, transcending the physical senses, as well as time and space. When we let our hearts be our eyes, ears and sense receptors, we experience a sense of knowing Love and God, which is beyond all measure.

You will know that you are taking the shortcut to God when right from the start, you follow your heart.

BEING IN THE PRESENCE OF CHILDREN

I delivered my first infant during my fourth year as a medical student at Stanford University School of Medicine in 1949. I was an atheist at the time but something happened in the delivery room that day that I will never forget.

children are often like wise, old spirits residing temporarily in young bodies, teaching me and the other volunteers Spiritual Truths.

In my heart I have felt that my life's work has been based on the biblical statement, "And a little child shall lead them." I have been blessed and honored by the trust and faith that these children have had in me. But even more, I have been blessed to witness the trust they have in a God they cannot see but whose presence gives them great comfort.

When we work with children their innocence soon reminds us our own innocence, and we realize that this state of being has never really left us.

Children have taught me honesty and integrity, for they instantly know who they can trust and whom they cannot. Their antennae are powerful and they quickly know who is deceiving them and who is being honest and real with them.

Young children live in the present. By living in the present they are much more forgiving then adults. Their enthusiasm for life and joy is unequaled.

Children are not so apt to get stuck in the past or the future, so being around them can teach us how to live in the present.

And that is where God is to be found—only in the present.

When you make time to be around children and learn from them; when you allow the little child in you to come out and play; when you choose to live each moment of your life with zest and joy; when you find yourself not looking at your watch to remind you of something in the future; when you focus only on the present moment; when you feel free to laugh a lot and to even be silly; when you have stopped taking yourself so seriously, then you can be mighty certain that you have found the shortcut to God.

To me, to be a messenger of love and a teacher of love is why we are here. Or to put it more simply, we are here to teach only love.

The *Manual for Teachers* in *A Course in Miracles* states that there are ten characteristics of God's teachers. These can be, in one sense, looked upon as landmarks that you will find along your pathway to God. I have paraphrased the following ten characteristics of God's teachers, drawn from *A Course in Miracles*[7]:

TRUST

As we approach the landmark of **Trust** on our journey to God, we find that this path is very different than the ego's where we encounter mountains of fear. Those mountains of fear rise out of distrust in all our relationships—with other people, with God, with ourselves, and with our own decision-making process.

On the shortcut to God the trust we find is based on our seeing only the Light of Spirit in each other as well as within ourselves, and knowing that the Light of Love and Spirit that we see never dies.

The landmark on the journey of the ego is distrust.

So when you say that you trust your brothers and sisters and see them as being at one with you, you are not talking about everyday behavior or actions. Rather, you are saying that you trust the Light of Love, the spirit that is in each person, that joins us as one, and that will always be there.

HONESTY

When you find yourself being consistently *Honest*, no longer using any form of deception of any kind, when you no longer find any value in being secretive, and there is a harmony in what you think, say, and do, you can be certain you are traveling on the road of love that will be the gateway to your Source.

TOLERANCE

The landmark we call *Tolerance* reminds us that we have let go of our judgments of each other and ourselves. When we are tolerant we can be reassured that we are traveling on the shortcut to our Higher Power. Without judgments we can see ourselves as equal with one another and acceptance becomes easy and natural.

GENTLENESS

The landmark of *Gentleness* reminds us that when this quality is in all our relationships it brings you closer to God. Gentleness in your soul becomes a reflection of the strength and the power of God's Love shining through you. In truth there is only gentleness in God and only gentleness in ourselves.

DEFENSELESSNESS

This landmark reminds us that we need never attack others, even though they might seem to attack us. *Defenselessness* is to everyone's advantage when we love rather than attack. When we know within our hearts that what we are is love and that we are always connected and at one with that which Created us, and that Love is the only reality there is, we also know that there is nothing that we need to defend.

The ego will tell us that our only reality is our physical body and that which we have made ourselves. To be defenseless is to remember that our true identity is as spiritual beings that can neither attack nor be attacked. Remembering this, we can choose differently and know that we are on the pathway to God.

When it appears that someone is attacking us, we can change our perception and remind ourselves that this person is really suffering from fear and lack of love and is giving a call of help. Being defenseless we can become messengers of love at such moments.

GENEROSITY

The landmark we call *Generosity* is different from the world's view of generosity. It has to do with spiritual generosity. It means that we place our highest value on that which is never diminished but is actually enlarged and expanded when we're giving it away. It reminds us that the only things of value are found in God.

Hence, giving and receiving are the same. The more love we give to others, the more love we receive.

PATIENCE

As you pass this landmark you will find that every person you meet on your life's path is a teacher of patience, reminding you that you are traveling through the land of *Patience*. You will then discover that the Infinite Patience of God is also your own attribute. The words "rush" and "hurry" will no longer be in your vocabulary and you will discover that Unconditional Love and Patience are one and the same.

FAITHFULNESS

The landmark of *Faith* reminds us that we can have faith in what we cannot see with our own eyes. Faith results when we transcend our belief that we are limited to a physical reality. It is a belief in something greater than ourselves that we experience only through our hearts.

OPEN MINDEDNESS

When we let go of judgments, expectations and assumptions, and the rigidity of the ego's thought system, we begin to receive the gift of flexibility and *Open Mindedness*. This landmark can put a spring into your step as you travel along the pathway to God.

When we have a willingness to be open minded, we

also open our hearts to forgiveness and to ending the illusion that we are separate from each other and our Creator.

JOY

This landmark reminds us that *Joy* and happiness are inevitable when we have trust, honesty, tolerance, gentleness, defenselessness, generosity, patience, faithfulness and open-mindedness within ourselves.

When we truly commit ourselves to love and trust in God, we recognize that happiness is our natural state, and that we deserve the right to be happy all of the time. When we let go of all of our judgments, laughter and joy become the music of our lives.

The landmark of the ego, by contrast, would have us being unhappy most of the time.

The coconut palm tree exemplifies this as it reaches up straight to the sun and the sky, yet is flexible and sways majestically in any storm.

When we let go of all of our judgments, laughter and joy become the music of our lives.

*Letting Go
and letting God
are one and the same.*

PART III

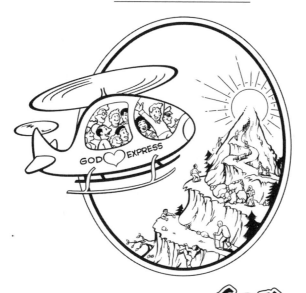

GOD ♥ EXPRESS

LESSONS for PERSONAL TRANSFORMATION

LESSONS FOR
PERSONAL
TRANSFORMATION

How To Proceed with the Lessons

The purpose of Part III is to present short lessons to help you experience the principles you've been reading about. Practicing these lessons will help you to gently release any blocks or hurdles that you may have unknowingly placed along your way to experiencing Love. When you open your mind and your heart, you will find that your soul is nourished and you will begin to sense a greater spiritual wholeness and fulfillment.

You may find some of the lessons difficult to accept, or you might have some difficulty seeing how they could be relevant for a particular problem in your life. This uncertainty does not really matter. What does matter is your willingness to practice the lessons without exception. The experience resulting from this practice can help you find Oneness in everything you do.

As you approach these lessons, remember that willingness to do them does not imply mastery. It only means that you have a readiness to change any misperceptions you might have about being separated from other people or from that power which is greater than any of us.

Here are six simple suggestions to assist you as you are reading these lessons for the first time and starting to practice them:

1.   Have a willingness to be open minded and to hold on to nothing.

2.   Be willing to respond to the word "God" as if you were seeing it for the first time in your life.

3.   Beginning with Lesson 1, experience one lesson each day, allowing them to become part of your being.

4.   You might wish to write the title of each lesson on a card and keep it with you throughout the day so that you can review it periodically and apply it.

5.   Before going to bed at night, relax and take a few moments to review the day's lesson. Ask yourself if you would be willing to have these ideas incorporated in to your dreams.

6.   When you have completed all of the lessons, your learning will be further facilitated if you begin again with the first lesson and repeat the entire series, again finding new ways that they can be applied in your everyday life.

LESSON 1

FORGIVENESS IS THE FASTEST SHORTCUT TO GOD

Forgiveness is the Fastest Shortcut to God

On this day may I find the value of forgiveness by letting go of any grievances I might have toward the world, God, and everyone else, including myself. May I remember that forgiveness can be a continuous process for me as long as I remain in this body. I shall let every breath I take and every footstep be toward forgiveness in every area of my life. Remind me that forgiveness erases the past, setting me free and bringing me the peace and happiness I seek.

Let me this day choose forgiveness to remove any bitter feelings, grievances and judgments since these keep me feeling weary, half dead and separate from God. May this be the day that I let go of all my judgments so that I may once again experience peace of mind.

Today I will choose to explore the possibility that if I am in pain and am suffering I might be holding on to some unforgiving thought. And I choose this day to let go of those thoughts and find freedom from my pain.

Example:

Throughout most of my adult life I have worked with people who were having difficulty in their relationships or in their feelings about themselves, and with children who were ill and facing the possibility of death.

In the past the field of medicine has tended to categorize patients as having either physical or emotional problems. In my experience of getting to know people in both these groups, there is little doubt in my mind that regardless of the illness, unforgiving thoughts usually play some role that inhibits the person from enjoying true well being.

Time and time again I have seen people who were suffering great physical pain, with diseases such as AIDS and cancer, where conventional pain medications seemed to do no good. When these people forgave old grievances from past relationships amazing things began to happen. Sometimes, drugs that had not given them any relief from their pain suddenly began to work. They breathed easier and seemed to gain the energy they needed to deal with their illness. With some people, pain seemed to subside with no medication at all.

I have been with a number of people during the last days of their lives and have learned so much from them. What I have noticed is that as we begin to look back on our lives we recognize that only one thing prevents us from experiencing inner peace. That one thing is our unhealed relationships.

Many courageous people that I have known have chosen to forgive their past grievances and to forgive

*"We do not remember God when
we're focused on our hurts of the past."*

themselves. They have told me that in doing this they feel a sense of relief and inner peace that they had never before experienced in their lives.

How blessed I have been to witness this moment with so many people. It is an amazing sight to behold, the transformation of angry eyes into peaceful ones.

We need to remind ourselves and each other that it is never too early, or too late, to forgive. In my book, *Forgiveness, The Greatest Healer of Them All*, I list many reasons why we don't forgive.

Not forgiving is a decision to suffer since in clinging to our grievances we continue to hang on to the toxic thoughts of anger and resentment that wreak havoc with our health. Furthermore, when I speak of forgiving, I am not speaking of condoning hurtful behavior or agreeing with a decision that I believe with all my heart is wrong. You are not releasing the person you feel has hurt you from accepting responsibility for whatever they might have done.

Forgiveness means giving up all hope for a better past. It is the elixir that erases the painful past so that we can begin to live in the present, where God is found.

Forgiveness heals our illusions of separation in the perceptual world of our daily lives. It releases us from the last obstacles preventing us from experiencing our Oneness with God. It is the bridge to peace and happiness, taking us right into the heart of God, where we have been all along.

LESSON 2

SMILES AND JOY WILL BE MY WAY TODAY

Smiles and Joy
Will Be My Way Today

This is the day that I choose to let joy be more important to me than fear.

Let me remember that joy is my natural state and is intertwined with love and peace, as one.

Help me to remember that it is my attachments to fear and my own judgments that get in the way, blocking me from experiencing my natural state, which is happiness.

Today I will hold within me a willingness to let go of my worries about the future and the fearful past by which I have blocked my awareness of joy and laughter.

This is the day of letting go of my ego, letting God take over, and lightening up.

Example:

Children are our best teachers. They are special angels, teaching all of us what love and joy are all about. We have much to learn from them about the

*"Laughter and happiness occur
when we let go of our judgments."*

spontaneity of laughter and joy. Perhaps the music of laughter comes much more easily to little ones than to grownups because they are much closer to their spiritual core.

One of the blessings of children is their inability to tell time by the clock. They have little understanding of words like "tomorrow" and "yesterday." They put their hearts and souls into living fully and joyfully in the present moment, as if time did not exist at all.

In so many ways, children are closer to the present than most adults because they allow themselves the luxury of being silly and gleeful, with few worries about what other people think. They have the spiritual wisdom to wake up and greet each new day with few concerns about tomorrow. Youngsters care little about completing the tasks on a "To Do" list. They make use of their ability to see everything as if for the very first time. Whether flowers or weeds, both are equally beautiful to them. Their discovery of each new creation in the garden of life fills them with wonder.

Unconstrained by "reality," children have the capacity to create imaginary friends to keep them company when they are lonely, or to invent games with their friends.

Small children have Faith and Trust, which provide the foundation for their joy. It is a joy coming from the fact that they do not take themselves too seriously.

I know so many adults who are considered "senior

"*Children are closer to the present
because they allow themselves the luxury
of being silly and gleeful.*"

citizens" who do not count their years but continue to be young at heart. They allow the playful child that is within their hearts to come out and play every day. They live in the present, free of judgment and open to each and every moment of life.

One of the lessons that children offer us in great abundance is that everyone can be our teacher, regardless of their age, and teach us the simple secrets of living a joyful life.

LESSON 3

I AM WILLING TO CONSIDER THE POSSIBILITY THAT I AM MORE THAN MY BODY

I am willing to consider the possibility that I am more than my body[2]

Today I will do my best to have a willingness to let go of all my beliefs about what I thought I was. No longer will I choose to let my rational mind and my physical senses determine what is real for me.

On this day I will consider the possibility that what is real has no physical form that can be measured or seen with my eyes, heard with my ears, felt by my touch, or even tasted or smelled.

Let me consider the possibility that my true identity is not a body but the Essence of Love, which never changes and is constant. Remind me that bodies continue to change, to come and go, but Love, which is never ending, is our true reality.

Let me consider the possibility that I was created by the Source that some call God, and that I am a Spiritual Being, a loving, formless force that is but temporarily housed in a physical body.

Example:

To remind ourselves of who and what we really are, Diane and I practice a spiritual exercise when, upon awakening in the morning, we hold hands and repeat the following prayer before getting out of bed. This prayer is from *A Course in Miracles*[8]:

> *I am not a body,*
>> *I am free*
>>> *For I am still*
>>>> *As God Created me.*
>>>>> *I want the Peace of God.*
>>>>>> *The Peace of God*
>>>>>>> *Is everything that I want.*
>>>>>>>> *The aim of all my living here,*
>>>>>>>>> *My purpose, my function, my life,*
>>>>>>>>>> *While I abide*
>>>>>>>>>>> *Where I am not at home.*

This exercise allows us to start the day reminding ourselves of who and what we are, created in the image of God and Love. It reminds us that we are spiritual beings here, holding the single goal of inner peace, the peace of God, throughout the day.

There are those days when we allow ourselves to get caught up in our egos and become fearful and judgmental. At those times we can simply start the day over again and let go of everything that happened before. To do this we find a place where we can be still and clear our minds of the clutter. It can be helpful then to recite the above prayer, reminding ourselves of our true identity, not as physical bodies but as spiritual beings.

Each time we remind ourselves of our true identity, it is like replacing the rudder in the boat that had been circling endlessly at sea. Suddenly, we are reminded of who we are and our course becomes clear.

LESSON 4

TODAY I WILL SEE EVERYONE AS MY TEACHER OF PATIENCE

Today I will see everyone as my teacher of Patience

Today I will remind myself that God has infinite patience—and so can I. I will remember that patience is an expression of love. God never holds a stop watch timing how long to be patient, and neither will I.

We can learn about God through all of our relationships. It is often true that we project our own impatience with ourselves into our relationships, thus becoming impatient with others and blaming or being judgmental of them. Perhaps the first step in being patient with others is to ask why we are so impatient with ourselves.

Learning patience is a shortcut to God that you can practice every moment of your life. If you are driving in your car, late for an appointment, or just in a rush, it is easy to get irritated and angry when the car ahead of you slows you down. But we can remind ourselves that we might also choose to see this driver as our teacher of patience.

If your spouse forgets to pick up the laundry or something at the supermarket when they said they would, love them and see them as your teacher of patience.

If your child misbehaves, resist the temptation to lose your temper. See your child as your teacher of patience.

If you are in a slow line at the supermarket or bank, see this as an opportunity for you to love the tellers and those people ahead of you, waiting in line.

"Today I will see everyone as my teacher of patience."

Example:

In 1988, a young man who was an architect asked me to come to his native country of Nicaragua. He wanted me to help him bring Christmas presents to the orphans of his country.

I accepted his invitation and was able to bring with me quite a few toys from the San Francisco Bay area. However, when I arrived at the Nicaragua airport, nobody was there to meet me, as we'd planned. For a while I seemed to be the only person at the airport.

The young architect had no phone, so I began to get quite impatient. I was thinking that maybe I should get back on the plane and return to the United States. I finally decided to stay.

I told myself that if ever there was a lesson in patience for me, this was a big one. My plane took off and there I was, alone at the airport.

I found a bench, relaxed, and decided that I had been given this time to relate to God. So I prayed, giving gratitude for all the blessings of my life. I was amazed by how relaxed and free of anxiety I became.

Three hours passed and my friend finally showed up at the airport. His car had broken down and it had taken him all that time to borrow a car to drive out and pick me up.

Sometimes, miracles follow periods of patience. During that trip, I tried unsuccessfully to phone Diane on Christmas day. A few hours later I was at the orphanage wearing a red Santa Claus hat and helping to hand out the presents I had brought for the children. There was a television crew there which I thought was from a local station. When I returned to the States, however, Diane said she saw me on CNN, giving out presents on Christmas day. So I had been able to get through to her after all!

Later, during my stay, I spent three hours talking with President Ortega, the president of Nicaragua at the time. We spoke about our relationship with God.

The following year, through our *Children as Teachers of Peace* foundation, Diane and I brought children to Nicaragua. They had an interview with Mr. Ortega, which was broadcast throughout the United States.

My willingness to be patient during that lonely three-hour wait at the airport proved to have many unexpected dividends.

LESSON 5

LOVE, WHICH IS WHAT I AM, REQUIRES NO DEFENSES

Love, which is what I am, requires no defenses[3]

Help me to look beyond the world that believes in defense and attack. And help me remind myself that anytime I defend myself from another person's verbal attack, I am actually attacking that person.

Help me live this day in defenselessness, letting the purity of my love be felt by all. Let me remind myself that when I know that my true identity is love I will also know that nothing can truly hurt me.

I am determined that on this day I will follow a path of love and defenselessness, neither attacking nor defending. Remind me to hold everyone's heart, including my own, gently.

Example:

I am writing this lesson while Diane and I are on a lecture tour in Australia. During this trip I was reminded of a previous lecture tour in this country. It was at that time that I had a most important lesson for learning the power of defenselessness.

On my previous tour I was talking about my book Love Is Letting Go of Fear, which had just been published in Australia. I was being interviewed by a radio talk show host who obviously did not like my book. He was attacking me all over the place.

After several minutes of this, I went into automatic ego mode and was tempted to defend myself and

"Let us hold each others' hearts gently."

attack him right back. Then I remembered the principles of Attitudinal Healing, and decided that he must be coming from a place of fear. I decided to send him love, to be defenseless, and not be concerned about whether his behavior changed or not.

The man continued to attack me verbally but I felt peaceful.

The next evening I was lecturing to about 2,000 people at Sydney's Town Hall. I looked down and who should I see in the front row but the same man who had been so vehemently attacking me on the radio the day before! I was puzzled about why he would come to my lecture. And I was also surprised to see that he seemed to be listening with genuine interest to what I had to say.

The next day the phone rang in my hotel room. I said hello and was again surprised to discover it was the same radio interviewer. He asked if he could see me about a problem he was having. We met later that day and spent two hours talking in my room. He was polite and kind through the entire visit and said that our discussion helped him to solve the problem he was facing.

As I look back on that experience, I think I might have been one of the few people he had ever known who didn't immediately launch a counter attack during an interview. And perhaps that was why he had decided to trust me.

I benefited from this experience because I saw that my defenselessness gave this man an opportunity to feel my love, and so ended up believing I was someone he could trust.

On this last trip to Australia that Diane and I made together we were scheduled to be on another radio program with another host that our friends had warned us about. We were told that this man frequently got brusque and even hostile with his guests. We went on the program holding the intent that we would be defenseless and would not attack him back.

During the program we got into a discussion about choices in our lives. I remarked that we could choose to listen to the Gandhi within ourselves. Diane added that we could also choose to listen to the Hitler within us.

Our host said that in the past he had been accused of being like Hitler, but nobody had ever suggested he might have a Gandhi within him. He then reflected, "You mean I really could choose to have a Gandhi inside me?" Diane and I emphatically said yes.

During the remainder of the interview our host's demeanor was peaceful and soft. As we left he thanked us and handed us a couple of his business cards. On one of them I penciled in a new middle name for him: Gandhi. I handed it back to him and he smiled as he went back on the air.

From that day on I have believed in the power of defenselessness and have felt that being defenseless is the way I would like to be all my life.

LESSON 6

THERE IS NO CRUELTY IN GOD AND NONE IN ME

There is no cruelty in God and none in me[4]

Today I will remember God by being determined to have only kind, loving, and gentle thoughts.

I will focus this day on being responsible for having no thoughts that would hurt others or that would be cruel to other people or myself. I will do this by remembering that there is no cruelty in God and thus there is no cruelty in me.

Example:

Until I turned fifty my life was pretty much dominated by my fears. I could be very loving and kind to my patients, but outside my office I could be awful. Although I tried very hard to put on a good front I was unhappy, angry and depressed. I had a reputation for being explosive and everyone tried to stay out of my way.

If I was angry nobody in the world could convince me it wasn't totally justified. It was my belief and perception that the person who had offended me deserved my hurtful remarks in return. I could be cruel beyond belief with both my words and my actions.

Soon after I began my spiritual journey I began to learn the value of forgiving myself and others. Soon, the depression and anger started to vanish. I finally realized that I could never experience the peace of

mind I so desperately wanted as long as I was hooked into what I considered to be my "justified anger."

I am convinced that much of our human behavior has at its roots in the beliefs we hold in our minds about God's identity. If we believe in a cruel, wrathful God who is sitting over us, judging our every thought, feeling, and action, we ourselves may become cruel, wrathful and judgmental in how we treat ourselves and others.

There are many different belief systems about God in the world. Sometimes these belief systems lead to religious wars fought in the name of God, with the belief that God tells us that it is okay to judge and reject certain people because of their behavior, or fight and even kill each other under certain circumstances. Related to this is the fact that there are many of us who are fearful of God, believing that God is somehow capable of hurting, killing or punishing us or other people in cruel ways.

Debate still goes on throughout the world about whether or not God is masculine, feminine, or genderless, and even if God exists at all.

But what if instead of being concerned about looking at God as judgmental, angry and cruel, or one gender or another, we were to look at the world in another way, believing that what created us is only a loving force. We can look upon our Source as a Loving Energy beyond our comprehension, a force of peace and joy, with a total absence of anger, cruelty, or desire to punish or hurt anyone. We can learn to forgive our misperceptions of a judgmental God.

Our true self is but a reflection of this Loving Force, where only love is found and nothing else. Our higher self, our spiritual self, is always at one with God, expressing only Love.

Our lower ego self, however, is capable of great cruelty. So it is important to know that we have a choice, that each of us is capable of retraining our minds to follow the way of peace rather than following the ego's guidance of fear, judgment and cruelty.

We can focus on listening to the voice of God instead of the ego. We can determine to be responsible for our own thoughts. We can choose to have only loving thoughts in our minds, resolved that we will not be cruel or hurtful to anyone.

LESSON 7

GOD GOES WITH ME WHEREVER I GO

God goes with me wherever I go[5]

It will be my intent to repeat this lesson throughout the day: "God goes with me wherever I go." I will do my best to resist the temptation of my ego's voice, which tells me that I am alone in the world, rejected, and abandoned.

When we truly believe there is no separation between ourselves and God, there is only Oneness, one joined mind. Then we not only have faith but we know that God goes with us wherever we go. A shortcut to God is found by taking a leap of faith and letting go of the belief that we are separate minds, knowing instead that we are all integral parts of a whole.

When we trust that God is within us wherever we go, we no longer feel abandoned or lonely. Our worries, anxieties and feelings of helplessness fade away. God's peace and our peace become one and the same.

The peace, love, and happiness we experience in our lives is a natural offshoot of recognizing that we are all joined with God. We can manifest and experience that peace regardless of the chaos that might be going on in our external lives.

When we live in the past, there are many times that we continue to suffer anxiety, fear, depression and a sense of helplessness because of our own feelings of inadequacy, lack of self-worth, attachments to anger, or self-condemnation. These feelings usually rise out

"When we choose to erase the past,
we then experience the presence of God."

of the often unrecognized emotions of believing we are alone and unloved. When we choose to erase the past, we then experience the presence of God.

When we change our belief system to accept that we are never alone but that God and God's abundant, unconditional Love is with us all the time, we find that our sense of separation vanishes and we experience the Oneness that is our birthright.

Example:

In May of 1996, Diane and I were invited to visit Iran. Five of our books have been published there and our Iranian friends had arranged for us to come and speak. Many of our friends suggested that it might be too dangerous to go there because of our government's conflicts and the anti-American feelings that had been reported by the media.

We were guided to accept the invitation to go there and speak. We were to let go of our fear and remember that God goes with us wherever we go.

Once we arrived in Iran we gave many talks in hospitals, universities, and for other groups. One of our first lectures was at the main psychiatric facility in Teheran. We were told that there would be no translator since most people there spoke English.

Just before we started our talk one of our hosts pointed to a man in the audience wearing a turban. He was a representative from the government and his job was to evaluate what we had to say. Our audience seemed very appreciative, but the man wearing the turban frowned, looked disgruntled, and even angry.

My ego went crazy as I imagined Diane and I being dragged off to jail for saying the wrong thing.

At that moment my spiritual principles went out the window. I felt abandoned by God and was sure that God was not there with me in Teheran. I started thinking that I should have listened to all those friends back in the States who told me not to make this trip.

Then I decided to ignore my ego's warnings and to perceive this man in the turban not as attacking me at all. I stopped trying to interpret his facial expressions. I pictured the Loving God within him as well as within me. The man's facial expressions didn't change but I became peaceful, feeling the presence of God within.

After we finished our talk, the professor who had invited us gave a ten-minute summary in Farci, the Iranian language, of what Diane and I had said. The audience applauded enthusiastically but the man in the turban barely clapped at all.

Later, I was surprised when the man in the turban came up to us with a huge smile on his face. Through the help of an interpreter he told us that he did not understand one word of English. With much animation he said that he fully agreed with all the principles we talked about, which had been summarized in Farci following our talk.

The lesson for me was that all the fear I had experienced when I watched this man's disapproving

expressions was due to my own misguided projec-
tions of what he was thinking. I had projected my own
fear to him.

LESSON 8

MAY THE GIFT
OF GENEROSITY
BE WITH ME
EVERY STEP
OF THE WAY

> *May the gift of generosity be with*
> *me every step of the way*

When I choose to give with no expectations and no attachments concerning the outcome, I begin to experience the core of my being as love, joy, and peace, all woven together as one. This happens the moment I wholly let go of all thoughts of getting anything in return, not even receiving a thank-you or other acknowledgement of what I have given.

I will concentrate on giving rather than getting, in everything that I do, carrying a single thought with every person I meet: "How can I be helpful?"

I will do my best to learn that giving and receiving are the same. We know we are on a shortcut to God when we have a willingness to let go of our ego's goals of possessiveness and ownership.

The moment we are willing to share what we have with others, giving with generosity, we begin to experience the law of Love—that giving is a gain and not a loss. That law is, of course, just the opposite of what the ego would have us believe.

Example:

I would like to share with you a story that people seem to like me to retell. A number of years ago I found myself lecturing in Santa Fe, New Mexico where I met a man named Ortega. This man's life work was making wooden sculptures of St. Francis of Assisi. For many years the prayer of St. Francis had been part of my daily ritual, so I fell in love with Ortega and his sculptures.

I purchased one of the sculptures for myself and slightly larger ones for Diane and my dear friend, Bill Thetford. Every morning, in front of my little statue, I would repeat the prayer of St. Francis.

Several years later I had a gathering at my house for the parents of children with cancer. One of the mothers became very attracted to the little sculpture. At the same time a little voice within my heart said, "Give the statue to her. It is the one thing in your house that you are still attached to."

I did give her the statue and it was a joy to do so. Then, about six months later, Diane and I were back in Santa Fe lecturing. After the lecture, it was announced that our host had a gift for us. I was filled with awe as we were presented with this miracle—an almost life-sized sculpture of St. Frances made by my friend Ortega.

We learned that day that giving is receiving in ways that we cannot even imagine. I had experienced a miraculous opening of my heart the moment I gave the little sculpture to the woman who had been a guest in my home. It had never occurred to me to expect anything more. Yet, there were lessons about

"May every footstep
I take be one of
Giving and
Generosity."

this that I was still to learn. Sometimes when you let go of what your ego may prize, your giving comes back to you in unimaginable ways, and this was one of those times. But the story doesn't end there.

In 1998 we were consulting at a conference on reconciliation and forgiveness in Bosnia where we met a priest from the order of St. Francis. This man had lost his church and was displaced. He and his congregation were holding Sunday services out in the open.

We shared with this priest our story about the St. Francis sculptures and Ortega and promised our new friend that we would send him one of Ortega's wonderful statues when we returned to the States.

Back home, we phoned Ortega to order a St. Francis sculpture to send to the priest, but we found out that Ortega had died and that his son had taken over the business. When the son found out where we were sending the sculpture, he insisted on giving it to us free of charge.

The energy of giving and receiving continues to gain momentum and to give new meaning to our lives.

May the gift of the joy of giving and generosity be with every footstep that I take and may it infect everyone around me.

LESSON 9

TENDERNESS AND GENTLENESS WILL BE MY WAY TODAY

Tenderness and gentlenesss will be my way today

When we find that we are not being gentle and tender in all of our relationships, it is a sign that we have lost our way and have separated ourselves from our Source.

The natural state of our hearts is gentleness and tenderness, and when we find that we are being brusque, tough, harsh, hard, and short with each other, we have become fearful and are listening to the voice of our ego and not the voice of Love.

Let us remember in every thought we have, and in everything we do, that tenderness and gentleness go together as an expression of the purity of God's Love, always residing within us. Let us remember that a shortcut to God is when tenderness and gentleness walk hand in hand.

Example:

When we are in the center of the flow of God's Love, tenderness and gentleness become a part of our natural state. It is only when we choose to listen to the voice of the ego and enter into a fearful state that tenderness and gentleness disappear.

Tenderness and gentleness are not limited to one gender or another. Unfortunately, many men still hold the belief that tenderness and gentleness might be

*"When Tenderness and Gentleness
walk hand in hand it becomes a Shortcut to God."*

viewed as only feminine and a sign of weakness. But just the opposite is true: Tenderness and gentleness are sources of strength, not weakness.

It is wonderful to see tough-minded professional athletes, such as football players, visiting the children's cancer ward and allowing their tenderness and gentleness come out, front and center. It is a reminder for all of us to demonstrate and be models of tenderness and gentleness not only for our children but for everyone we meet.

It is my belief that one of the many reasons that we find babies so precious is that their tender, and gentle natures remind us of our spiritual essence.

We might be tense and angry, but when we hold a newborn infant our anguish or anxiety are washed away completely by the purity of love found in the baby's presence, there within our arms. Who can hold a newborn and not experience the miracle of birth, the scent of innocence, tenderness, and gentleness?

Throughout our lives it can be most helpful to remember that people who may seem angry and have a loud bark may be suffering from lack of love. They do not need our anger or our fear, but they are calling out for help. Our love, our tenderness, and our gentleness are often the way to answer their call for help and open their hearts.

LESSON 10

THIS IS A DAY
FOR ME
NOT TO BE
IN A HURRY

This is a day for me not to be in a hurry

Let me remind myself today that God is never in a hurry and that I can live each moment in a timeless way. There is no reason to be in a hurry when I know I am already home in God's Heart.

Help me to not be in a hurry but to spend this day in slow motion as I listen to others, when I share my love with others, when I am talking, when I am eating, when I am walking, and when I am meditating, praying and thinking about God.

Example:

When I was a kid it seemed like everything my family did was done in a hurry. My folks had a small date shop that opened to the street. Our modest house was down an alley behind the store.

We always had dinner at 5:00 in the evening and were finished eating by 5:15. Whether I was eating, doing the dishes, mowing the lawn, going to bed, or whatever I was doing, I kept hearing the words from my parents, "Hurry up!"

When I grew up to be an adult I was always in a hurry, too. Frankly, I was often confused about whether I was running away or running toward something. I lived my life on a treadmill turned up to its highest speed. Most of the time I was breathless, but I

"Practice not being in a hurry."

did not know how to get off that endless cycle I found myself on.

I am convinced that I am not alone in these feelings. I am sure that thousands upon thousands of people have chosen to speed along in the fast lane, hurried through life by their fear. This lane is definitely not a shortcut to God. It is also known as the "ego lane."

Since I began my spiritual journey in 1975 I have begun to see more value in living an unhurried life, of getting up earlier and starting the day gently, softly taking time to experience the Presence of God.

Perhaps the secret of changing any behavior is to no longer value the old behavior but to begin valuing the new. The moment we begin to value being in the quiet, unhurried presence of God, we will begin to experience the inner peace we have been seeking.

LESSON 11

I WILL BE
HONEST IN
EVERYTHING
I DO

I will be honest in everything I do

Let me be reminded that it is easy to develop honesty when we are centered in Love and let our lives be guided by our devotion to a Higher Power. From this, there naturally evolves a foundation built on a bedrock of Truth.

What is honesty and integrity but having harmony in everything we think, say, and do? We develop honesty by not holding conflicting goals within our minds and by having the single goal of inner peace.

When we find ourselves lying or deceiving other people or ourselves, when we have put on smiling masks and are speaking pleasant words, when we are actually full of anger, we can be sure that we are not being honest. We are motivated by fear, not love, and have forgotten our focus on Love and God.

Let me focus this day on honesty and integrity in all of my relationships. Let this be a day when I keep all my agreements, a day completely without lies or deceptions of any kind. Let me make this day one in which Truth becomes the rudder and keel of my ship, holding a steady course on my journey to God.

Example:

Honesty applies in the little things as well as the big things in life. There is no such thing as being "fairly honest" or "a little dishonest."

A number of years ago I went to Poland to inter-view Lech Walesa for my book *One Person Can Make A Difference*. I found that he was some distance from the capitol, so I hired a taxi and arranged for an inter-preter.

Upon my return to Warsaw following the interview, the cab driver offered to make out a false bill showing that I had paid more for my fare than I actually had. He said that I could use it to get a larger deduction on my income tax back in the States.

I thanked him and attempted to explain to him that if this conversation had taken place ten years before I would have been completely delighted and grateful for his offer. But on my present spiritual path I want-ed to live with total honesty and integrity. So I asked him to please make out the correct bill.

He began to argue with me, telling me why I should accept the inflated bill. I wasn't sure how to respond to him. Then I noticed that he had a little Crucifix hanging from the mirror of his car.

I asked him to imagine that this was not Dr. Jampolsky sitting in his car, but Jesus. Would he encourage Jesus to be dishonest?

Suddenly the driver understood my message. His face lit up with a big smile and he thanked me for the lesson in honesty. I then thanked him for teaching me to resist temptation because from my ego's point of view this idea of his had been a very enticing offer.

I got out of the cab with a feeling of gratitude for a new friend and the lesson that had been offered to me that day. I also felt grateful for resisting the temptation. I walked toward my hotel saying thank you, and feeling the closeness of God within my soul.

*"Let each moment of this day
be a timeless one."*

ings of people just sitting together with big smiles on their faces, not talking but just sharing the silence and their love for each other.

In their daily lives there was much more cooperation than competition. The movements of their lives seemed relaxed, flowing smoothly and slowly.

Music and dancing are particularly important for

"*I am
the Light
of the world.*"

I am the Light of the world [6]

Would you be willing to believe for a moment that there is a light beyond this physical world, which is brighter than any Earthly light? It is brighter, more loving, more beautiful, and more powerful than any you have ever seen with your eyes.

Would you be willing to consider that there is a Light Source —an Energy that created all life, and that you and I and everyone on Earth are part of it?

Would you, for just an instant, believe that you are a reflection of this Light and that you are the Light of the world, here to receive from your Source, to be that Light, and to shine the Light of Love upon all who you touch?

Allow the following words to slowly take form on your lips as you say to yourself, in a gentle whisper, "I am the Light of the world. I am here to shine the Light of Love on everyone, excluding no one."

Example:

I need all the help I can get to remind me that I am more than my body, that I am the Light, and that my Light is a reflection of God's Light.

There is a simple exercise that I do to remind me of who I am. I would like to share it with you. It goes like this:

Begin by imagining for a few moments that there is

no physical world or universe as you know it. There is nothing but emptiness, vast, endless emptiness.

Next, imagine that this emptiness is suddenly filled only with Light. There is nothing but Light, filling an eternal now, where there is no physical world, no time, space or form.

Now imagine that you are the Light which fills this emptiness. Imagine it until you are developing that inner knowledge, which you feel with all your heart, that you are this Light.

The next step is to imagine, for just an instant, that a physical world comes into being. Now you, as the Light, decide to materialize as a physical body with an ego. As you do this, touch your feet to the earth. Experience your Light going to all parts of the universe as you extend your Light of Love to all, if only for one second.

After you have done this, let your body dematerialize, merging with the universal Light again in a world that is only Light.

We can do this exercise over and over again. We do this exercise in order to remind ourselves that we are Light that is temporarily housed in our physical bodies.

A shortcut to God is to remember that all we ever have to do, one second at a time, is to shine our Light on all, seeing the Light of Love in everyone we behold, and knowing that this light is a reflection of ourselves.

LESSON 14

I REST
IN GOD

I Rest in God

Help me to remember that we can always put our ego aside for a moment and rest in the quiet, stillness of God, whose Peace is always there for us. I shall remember today that when I choose to rest in God my tired mind disappears and I find myself with renewed energy to go on.

We live in such a busy, noisy world. Each day we are bombarded by news on TV, the radio, and in newspapers about crises and disasters everywhere. The media itself is filled with programs and articles that make it very easy, and even tempting, for us to get caught up in the noise and chatter of the world.

There is a quote in *A Course in Miracles* that I find is a gentle reminder to me when I feel tempted to get caught up in the turmoil and busyness of the world:

"We ask for rest today, and quietness unshaken by the world's appearances. We ask for peace and stillness, in the midst of all the turmoil born of clashing dreams. We ask for safety and for happiness, although we seem to look on danger and on sorrow." [9]

The world of the ego frequently seems insane and unfair, full of conflict, chaos, danger, sorrow, and suffering.

There is a place of awareness in our hearts, a safe haven where we can find inner peace, and if we choose to believe, a place where the Peace of God resides. It is a place where we can rest and feel the gentle stillness and serenity of God's Love. All hell can break loose around us and we can rest safely in the arms of God, unaffected by the turmoil.

The spiritual reality of God never changes and is always available to us regardless of what is happening in the world around us. The perceptual reality of the ego, however, is constantly changing, stimulated by all the activities of the world.

Today I will rest in God and let my soul be bathed in the Light of that which Created me. It is in the stillness that I will find the Truth of God's unconditional love.

Help me to listen this day to the silence and gentle voice of Love. It is here that I can trust that I will receive all the guidance I will ever need about what to think, say and do.

Example:

What I have learned about being with other people when they are faced with death or catastrophic illness has helped me to also meet the challenges of my daily life and our frequently chaotic and distressing world.

While working with people who are facing serious illness and death, I discovered that finding peace of mind is most important to them. Over the years, I have learned that there is no pat formula for what to say or do. What has been most helpful to me, as well as to the people around me, is to take the time to quiet my mind and rest in God before visiting with the person who is dying.

What I have experienced is that the biggest gift I can give myself or another person, even under these difficult circumstances, is my own inner peace and the Presence of God that I am experiencing within my heart. More often than not, this is done without speaking any words, though whatever words we do speak come from the place of peace that is within us.

When I go within to ask for guidance about what I should think, say or do, the reply I most often get is, "Just be." Time and again I have found a depth of Love in the silence that is beyond my comprehension.

Simply holding another person's hand and seeing him or her in the Light has proved to be among the most uplifting, joyful, and meaningful experiences in my life. I have learned that often the most meaningful communication of all is felt in the silence. In fact, words often hinder this communication.

Resting in God energizes my soul and reminds me of my sacredness and of my own Oneness with all there is.

LESSON 15

LET ME
REMEMBER THAT
I AM ONE
WITH GOD

Let me remember that I am one with God [9]

Let me remember that I am One with God. Help me let go of my old belief system where my illusion is that we are separate and Oneness is impossible. Let me look past the world of form and its seemingly separate parts.

Open my mind and my heart, that I might exper ience the sweetness of Your unconditional Love, knowing that I can never be separate from You or Your Love.

Perhaps one of the biggest problems facing humankind is the spiritual amnesia that separates us from each other and from our Source. This illusion is based on the belief that our identities are limited to our physical bodies and that only money and material things will make us happy or allow us to feel secure. We may also feel that there is either no God or that God is vengeful and will punish us or do hurtful things.

When we are willing to transcend the world of perception, when we let the past be forgiven, when we choose to have only the loving thoughts of God in our minds, we begin to feel whole again.

On this day, let me feel Your Light, Peace, and Joy abiding in me. Remind me to feel Oneness with everyone I meet. May Your Will and my will be One.

Example:

While I was at Stanford Medical School, I met Arnie Beisser, who became one of my closest friends. Just before beginning his internship, Arnie discovered he had polio. His illness progressed quickly and he was soon confined to an iron lung.

As soon as I heard about his illness, I flew to Southern California where he was living at the time. It was difficult for me to see my friend, this wonderful, vibrant person with whom I had played tennis many times, confined first to an iron lung and later to a wheel chair. In a crazy way, there was a part of me that felt guilty that I was healthy and strong, while he was sick and possibly facing death.

In the beginning I was doubtful that he would make it. But Arnie proved me and everyone else around him wrong.

Though quadraplegic, Arnie continued to get better. In time he married his occupational therapist, Rita. As his health continued to improve, he went on with his schooling, became a psychiatrist, and even rose to be head of the Metropolitan State Hospital in Southern California. Later he was head of psychiatry for Los Angeles County.

During his career as a professor of psychiatry at UCLA, he wrote several books and always maintained a brilliant sense of humor.

In the years soon after the onset of his illness, I noticed that few of his classmates stayed in touch with him. I think they feared that if something like this could happen to Arnie it could also happen to them. It is not easy to accept how fragile and vulnerable the human body really is.

One of the greatest gifts I have received in life was having Arnie as my closest friend. From the time he came down with polio until the day he died, forty years later, we talked on the phone at least once a week and saw each other two or three times a year. Arnie enjoyed my calls from far off places like China, Australia, Argentina, and Russia. He saw the world from my heart and eyes, and he allowed me to see his world from one of the biggest hearts on Earth.

In my mind Arnie was a very spiritual person though he rarely used the word "God" or any other religious terminology. His life was filled with Spirit and Unconditional Love. With all the physical disabilities that he had, he was one of the most compassionate and caring people I ever knew. He taught me so much. I felt comforted every time I was with him to experience the deep Presence of God. Arnie died in 1991.

Looking back, I do believe that God had specially assigned us to one another so that we could experience that depth of Love that takes place between two friends who love each other with purity and integrity beyond anything imaginable.

We continue to feel at one with Arnie's spirit and with God, knowing that we joined forever.

LESSON 16

MAY THE LIGHT OF GOD IGNITE A FIRE WITHIN OUR HEARTS

May the Light of God ignite a fire within our hearts

With all my heart, mind, and soul, I open the door for God to ignite the Fire of Love within me. This Fire is aching to be released, full of passion, joy, and the energy of the highest and most Holy Inspiration, filled with the zest of being fully alive with Love that comes from knowing that I am always in the Center of God's Heart.

Let my only hunger, thirst, and desire be to receive and bathe in the Love of the Divine. May the rapture and fire of Creation's Love explode and radiate through every pore of my being, that I may be a vehicle helping to ignite this same fire in everyone I meet or even think about.

Let me remember that when I open the door to a Loving God who knows no judgments, I can experience the Flame of Love's Creation that will never go out.

It is only by forgetting my true identity that I block my awareness of the Flame of Love from our Source. That Flame can never, ever disappear, though I may block my awareness of it.

Let me be free forever of the fear that causes me to shrink from Love, turning my heart to stone and erecting a picket fence around it. I know that I can find this freedom simply by accepting my role as Your messenger of Light, Love, Peace, and Joy.

Let our smiles of knowing who and what we are circle the entire universe, bathing all in the Light of Love that we each help to illuminate.

Example:

Diane and I recently completed a lecture tour on Attitudinal Healing that took us to Sydney, Tasmania, Bundanoon, and Perth, Australia.

On the evening of our last night of the trip, we were asked by our young friend Meneesha Michalka to have a dialogue with her youth group, which meets every Sunday night at her Church. Mineesha's parents started the Center for Attitudinal Healing in Perth.

We have known Meneesha since she was five years old and we call her our adopted Australian daughter. In a most beautiful way, Meneesha has incorporated Attitudinal Healing principles into her life.

It was a most deepening experience for Diane and me to hear the heartfelt expressions of the struggles of these young people who were on spiritual paths.

Our meeting with the children reminded me that we hear so much in the media about young people who are either antisocial or leading very troubled lives. We seldom hear about the wonderful and exciting things that so many young people are doing. Many are striving to be kind, loving, and helpful in their communities all over the world.

Before going to the meeting with the children,

Diane and I prayed. We had been lecturing for days and were feeling tired that night. We asked for divine help, for the fire and passion of God's Love to ignite our hearts and spark our energy so that we might be helpful when we were with these young people.

As we entered the room where the meeting was to take place, we suddenly felt ourselves filled with energy and inspiration. We started by saying that if we believed it, this evening could be one of the most important evenings of our lives. We could experience peace of mind beyond anything we had experienced before.

We shared inspiring stories about people we have met in our travels who are truly making a difference in the world. We spoke of how each one of us has the potential to make a positive difference in the world. We talked about ways we can remove the blocks to experiencing God's Love.

As I spoke that night, I felt that same Light of Love, devoid of all judgments, radiating from me to everyone in the room. I then felt their Light and Love coming right back to me.

We spoke about not giving our power away to others, whether it is our parents, siblings, teachers, friends, or strangers—because we are the only ones who can make the decision to be happy. And we spoke of how important it is to let go of our judgments of others and ourselves.

LESSON 17

MAY THE WORD "GOD" BE ON MY LIPS THROUGHOUT THIS DAY

May the word "God" be on my lips throughout this day

I will awaken my consciousness to God today. I will focus on having a one word prayer, a one word mantra, that I will say over and over again in my mind: God.

I will see the word God everywhere that I look.

I will see the word God in my mind, in my heart and in the clouds.

I will feel the word God in every cell of my body, in every thought, and in every breath that I take.

I will be aware of the Presence of God in everyone I meet today.

I will devote this day to remembering God.

Example:

About fifteen years ago, Diane and I were lecturing in Japan. We had a couple free hours one afternoon, so we went to the park where we had a most remarkable experience.

A number of elderly women were sweeping leaves off the pathways through the park. One of them stood out from the rest. Her face was lit up with a smile full of joy that would melt anyone's heart.

Diane and I both had the impression that this woman swept with a certain passion, as if her work

"Sweeping can be a sacred experience."

was a special privilege rather than a required task. It was as if she was sweeping as a special favor to God. She carried herself regally, each stroke of her broom almost artful, like a dancer.

We were fascinated, almost hypnotized, watching her. We looked around. It seemed to be an ordinary park, nothing special. Yet, this woman made it a special place. To be in her presence was a holy encounter. It was as if, with each stroke, she was saying thank you to God for the privilege of sweeping a pathway to a place of worship.

Finally our curiosity got the better of us and we found someone who could translate for us so that we could have a conversation with her.

What we had sensed in watching her turned out to be true. She told us in a most simple and clear way that in her mind, sweeping this pathway was a special assignment from God. She did it with joy in her heart...grateful to serve God in this way, and to experience God's joy and love.

Many of us know that it can be helpful to think about God at special times during the day. This is more commonly done at night when we go to bed, during meals, or upon waking up in the morning. But what about the rest of the day?

In many contemplative spiritual groups even the most mundane tasks, such as washing dishes, cleaning floors, or digging a ditch, are sanctified by focusing on God as the person works. Diane and I have made even cleaning the bathroom or taking out the garbage holy, by thinking about God while we do it.

It is possible to have God on our mind throughout the entire day, regardless of our activities. We can do this on the subway, while driving to work, while standing in line at the supermarket. We can do it while walking and during athletic activities.

It is possible for us to make every activity in our lives a holy and sacred experience, remembering God's Love with a passion for compassion in every moment of our lives.

LESSON 18

LET ME
REMEMBER
TO SPEND TIME
IN NATURE

Let me remember to spend time in nature

A shortcut to God is to make it a priority to spend more time in nature. It is in nature that we discover the interconnectedness of all life. We learn how one form of life interweaves with another. A leaf drops off a tree and eventually it disintegrates, becoming energy that we cannot see with our physical eyes. The form changes but the life energy goes on.

Nature's influence in our lives can slow us down and give us a chance to appreciate the beauty and the serenity that are God's gifts to us. Being in nature gives us an opportunity to heal our perceptions so that even a weed that we might have previously thought of as ugly now can be perceived as such a beautiful Creation of God that it takes our breath away.

Let us this day choose to see the world through the lens of nature and rediscover our relationship with God and all that is sacred.

Example:

A number of years ago I made a decision to spend a full month on a retreat in Australia. There was part of me that was threatened and did not like the idea of being out of communication with Diane and the outside world.

During the retreat I was alone most of the time with my thoughts, deep in the heart of the natural wonder that is Australia. I did not read, write, listen to the radio, or watch TV.

I communicated with nature the whole month, which is another way of saying I communicated with God, to a depth I had never before experienced. I think there was a part of me that was afraid to be alone with my thoughts. It may seem odd to you, but what I missed for the first few days was my "To Do" list.

As time went on, I immersed myself in gardening, my fingernails becoming quite dirty each day. I took long hikes, feeling blissfully connected with nature and with God. I found myself carrying on conversations with trees and hugging them every day.

That month the whole rhythm and pulse of my life changed, slowing down dramatically. I was able to look into my heart and mind to get feedback on things that I had been too busy to experience.

There is something about the rhythm of nature that brings us back to our Source, reminding us of how important it is to get away from the busyness of the day.

I discovered that I had been *sort of* committed to God, mostly when it suited me, but I had not really taken that giant step of being totally committed to a life where God's Will and mine could become one.

There were many lessons for me during this retreat but one in particular stands out. It was a lesson in letting go that occurred on a hot afternoon after I had hiked out and found a magnificent rock in the middle of a slow-moving stream. I perched on this rock, watching the stream and the trees around me.

I had been there about an hour when I found myself concentrating on one small leaf on a branch of a tree above me. Suddenly, the leaf let go and fell into the stream. The wind caught it and it spun in a circle. Then, to my utter surprise it gently landed on the rock right next to me.

As I looked at my new friend, the leaf, it occurred to me that this was no accident and that I had something important to learn. I started to laugh at myself as I felt that the lesson for me that day, from this wise leaf, was to trust in the process and not be fearful of letting go. And, believe me, there were so many things that my ego was reluctant to let go of!

After about ten minutes, a gust of wind came up and the leaf was lifted high into the air, then it landed in the steam. The leaf was not fighting the current but was fearlessly going with the flow, full of trust.

I was reminded of how many times in my life I was full of fear about letting go and the times I was resistant to change and filled with distrust.

For me this dramatic lesson was to let go of all of my fear about trusting God and to totally trust the process of letting Go and letting God.

When I returned to California—to everyone's surprise and especially my own—I decided to take six months off from everything and do only gardening in my own back yard. Being with nature proved to be a most powerful, transformative experience for me.

The way to Peace
is to stop worrying
and put the future
in the hands of God.

PART IV

REFLECTIONS and MEDITATIONS

REFLECTIONS AND MEDITATIONS

Pathways of the Heart

I have had my ups and downs finding the short-cuts to God in my own life. There have been moments when I felt the bliss and awe of God's Presence. But I have also had my fights with God—at least, that is the way I sometimes perceived it.

Along the way I have found it most helpful to write about my feelings. I have particularly found this writing to be helpful in letting go and moving past obstacles that I put in the way of my experiencing God's Presence.

I have found some of my writing to be extremely helpful as meditations, reminding me of who I am. In the following pages I share with you some of these writings. It is my hope that if you like to write you might be inspired to express some of your own thoughts and feelings in this way.

My Fiery Anger

What is this cancer inside me?
The fiery anger that lingers,
In its thin disguise...
The coldness and brittleness
That bursts from my pores   .
At a moment's notice.

Could it all be fear,
And nothing but fear?
Is there no road map
That can lead me to peace
And freedom?

Can I really feel
Whole and at one
By simply crossing
The bridge of forgiveness?

Why does something
That seems so simple
Bring out my greatest
Resistance?

(continued)

My Fiery Anger (continued)

Obstacles, obstacles, obstacles!
Is that all there is to life—
A series of obstacles
Separating me from others?

When will I awaken to
The full awareness
That all obstacles
Between me and others
Are self-imposed?

I will then know that
I have manufactured them
Through my own fear of Love
And my own fear of God.

Letting Go

Help me to let go of my preoccupations
    with the future.
Give me the strength to stop
    my futile attempts
    to predict and control the future.
Let me see no value in my plan
    of what the future should be.

Rid me of my senseless questions
    about tomorrow
And of all my desires to manipulate
    and control others.
Remind me that my fears and uncertainties
    of tomorrow are only related to
    my unfounded fear of You.

Help me to be still,
    help me to listen and love.

Awaken me to the truth of Your Presence
    being only in the now of this moment.
Lift me up into Your Arms and
    remind me that I am Your Creation,
    and that I am the Perfection of Love.

Help me to acknowledge that I am
Your Messenger of Love,
    and free me to shine
    Your Light everywhere.

Choose Once Again

When my very foundation
  seems to have disappeared,

When there seems to be a serious question
  about meeting my basic needs of food and rent;

When my future seems to be in terrible doubt
  and the world seems very unfair;

When my heart feels it is skipping beats,
  and I am having trouble catching my breath;

When it feels that I am in shock …and that
  someone has punched me in the stomach, and
    when diarrhea seems to be the flow of the day;

When it feels that it is no longer safe to trust
  and that there is a temptation for me to blame
    someone else for the predicament I am in.

When I feel fragmented, as if I were a jig saw
  puzzle that has been thrown up into the air,
    feeling that it is impossible to be put
        back together again;

When it feels as if God has lost my file
  and has abandoned me, and that all my
    previous faith and trust was wrongly placed,
      and that I will never be able to trust
          or have faith in others or God again;

When I have forgotten that the essence of my being
  is Love, I can be absolutely sure of one thing—

It is not that God has abandoned me
  but that I have abandoned God ...

And I can choose once again.

A Fire Within My Heart

There is a fire of compassion within my heart,

A bubbling up of Love within my soul,

A vibration within every cell of my body,

A song of angels within my mind,

A call of Love from God within my being,

Saying,

Love, Love, Love, Love, Love.
As the Light of the world,

As a messenger of God's Love,
That is all you ever need do.

I AM

I am the Will of God.

I am the purity of love, joy,
  and peace united as one.
I am the essence of giving and joining.
I am the state of mind
  where there is
  total absence of fear, guilt,
  anger and hate, pain and sickness,
  judgment and separation of any kind.
I am the reflection of God's Love,
  and thus, I am everywhere;
  I have no boundaries and no form.

I am the Light of the world,
  and hence, the reflection of all
  that is beautiful.
I am a reflection of the simplicity of
  the flowers, the sand on the beach,
  the singing of the birds,
  the sound of the waves on the shore,
  and the stillness of the lake.
I am a reflection of all that
  is gentle, kind, tender, compassionate,
  and of all that is trusting and honest.

(continued)

I Am (continued)

I am that state of mind
   where there is only eternal life,
   and there is no death, and
   where there is only happiness.

I am the essence of Spirit, and it is my
   spiritual being that is my true identity.
I am whole and united with all life.
I am invisible and immeasurable.
I am God's Holy Child of Life;
I am God's Creation; God is my Cause
   and I am God's Effect.
I am co-creator of Love with God.
God's Will and my will are One.
If ever I accept anything else as my will
I deny what I am.

I am a reflection of the Will of God.

Surrender

And I asked, "What is the secret of
total surrender to God?"

And I was told,
   "The secret of surrender is simply
   to be.
The secret of surrender is simply
   not to think.
It is letting perception gently
   dissolve into the knowledge of Love,
   the land of no change,
   the Kingdom of God.
It is hearing the waves tenderly
   kiss the surf,
   becoming united, becoming one.
It is perception dissolving
   into knowledge of the perfect,
   One-essence of God and Love.

The secret of surrender is simply
   to do nothing and to be."

What is Beyond?

On this day the experience of my soul
   is beyond words.

What is beyond all feelings,
   beyond certainty and knowing
   that has no room for doubt?

What is beyond all limits
   and knows no barriers or boundaries?
What is beyond that which is
   all beautiful, magnificent and wonderful?

What is beyond the sunrise, the sunset,
   the moon and the sky
What is beyond all feelings of Love's abundance,
   of having no needs, with my heart brimming
   over with love?

What is beyond contentment,
   a feeling of well being,
   total happiness and joy
What is beyond the splendor
   and the magic of nature?

What is beyond the fullness of spirit
   that comes from the consciousness of giving?
What is beyond total trust,
   faith and commitment?
What is beyond Oneness, joining, and
   a state of no separation?

What is beyond feeling safe
   and knowing I will never
   be abandoned?
What is beyond the infinity of
   my passionate feelings of gratitude
   for all the Love I continue to receive?

What is beyond awe,
   mystery,
   and wonderment
   is

God's Love for me
   and
   My Love for God.

EPILOGUE

A Shortcut to God Is...

A Shortcut to God is...
Letting go of interpreting other people's behavior,
Letting go of all our judgments,
Letting go of our control issues,
Letting go of guilt, blame and shame,
Letting go of making others wrong
     and ourselves right,
Letting go of our expectations and
     our scripts for others,
Letting go of our assumptions,
Letting go of seeing the shadows of the past
     in others and in ourselves,
Letting go of all our unforgiving
     and self-condemning thoughts.

A Shortcut to God is...
Having the same interest in others
     as we have in ourselves,
Choosing to have peace of mind,
     and the Peace of God as our only goal,

Having a fire in our hearts
     to surrender to Love,
Knowing that our identity is the essence of Love
     and that we are no longer fearful of death.
Choosing peace instead of conflict,
Choosing to cooperate rather than compete,
Believing that giving is receiving,
Knowing that Love is the answer to every problem
     that we will ever face.

A Shortcut to God is...
Trusting and having faith in a
Loving, non-judgmental God,
Stepping aside and letting our Higher Power
     lead the way,
Putting the future in the hands of God,
Knowing that we are always loved by God.

A Shortcut to God is...
Knowing that when we've done all of the above,
Eternal peace, love, joy and happiness,
     will be ours.

All Endnotes from A Course in Miracles

1. Workbook for Students, Lesson 170, p. 326
2. Workbook for Students, Lesson 63, p. 63
3. Workbook for Students, Lesson 61, p. 102
4. Workbook for Students, Lesson 109, p.197
5. Workbook for Students, Lesson 124, p. 222
6. Workbook for Students, Lesson 188, p. 357
7. Manual for Teachers, pp. 9-16
8. Workbook for Students, Lesson 205, p. 390
9. Workbook for Students, Lesson 109, p. 197

Other books by Gerald G. Jampolsky, M.D.

Love is Letting Go of Fear
•
To Give Is to Receive: An Eighteen Day Mini-Course
on Healing Relationships
•
Teach Only Love: The Twelve Principles
of Attitudinal Healing
•
Good-bye to Guilt:
Releasing Fear through Forgiveness
•
Out of Darkness into Light:
A Journey of Inner Healing
•
One Person Can Make a Difference:
Ordinary People Doing Extraordinary Things
•
Forgiveness:
The Greatest Healer of All

With Diane V. Cirincione, Ph.D.

Love Is the Answer:
Creating Positive Relationships
•
Change Your Mind, Change Your Life:
Concepts in Attitudinal Healing
•
"Me First" and Gimme Gimmes: A Story of Love
and Forgiveness, Choices and Changes
•
Wake-Up Calls

With Lee L. Jampolsky, Ph.D.
Listen to Me: A Book for Men and Women About
Father-Son Relationships
•

AUDIOCASSETTES

Forgiveness Is
the Greatest Healer of All
•
Love is Letting Go of Fear
Teach Only Love
•
Good-Bye to Guilt
•
To Give Is to Receive
•
Love Is the Answer;
Creating Positive Relationships
•
Forgiveness Is the Key to Happiness
•
Introduction to
A Course in Miracles
•
One Person Can Make a Difference
•
The Quiet Mind
•
Achieving Inner Peace
•
Visions of the Future
•
Finding the Miracle of Love
in Your Life; Based on A Course in Miracles

VIDEOCASSETTES

Achieving Inner and Outer Success
•
Healing Relationships
•
Visions ofthe Future

For information about the CENTER FOR ATTITUDINAL
HEALING in Sausalito, California, and its workshops,
or about other centers, or about the lectures and
workshops of Jerry Jampolsky and Diane Cirincione,
please contact The CENTER FOR ATTITUDINAL HEALING,
33 Buchanon Drive, Sausalito, CA 94965;
phone (415) 331-6161; fax: (415) 331-4545.
website: www.healingcenter.org.
email: home123@aol.com

If you wish to purchase books and audio- or video-
tapes, please contact Miracle Distributions,
1141 East Ash Ave., Fullerton, CA 92631;
phone; 1-800-359-2246;
or contact
The CENTER FOR ATTITUDINAL HEALING,
SAUSALITO, CALIFORNIA